Deep Love Within

Vic Hall

Michael Terence
Publishing

First published in paperback by
Michael Terence Publishing in 2020
www.mtp.agency

ISBN 9781913653170

To my two daughters Michelle and Natalie, your love is so precious to me and a joy and inspiration to others…

no father could be more blessed.

Thank you for your inspiration and love in compiling these beautiful poems.

Love your brother and sister as I have loved you.
For love is the breath and joy of life.

Contents

A Beautiful Dream

There are oceans that are wide and deep
I see them, as I see you in dreams of sleep,
Like the sun up above, a warm smile appears
Of happiness and contentment down the years.

Of fun and laughter, notes and photographs kept
Of friendship, love, in writing quite adept,
Loyalty and sincerity, fun and jokes to admire
Your sense of humour of which I will never tire.

The warmth of your love, romantic with feeling
You are a being of intense passion so appealing,
In my dreams your spirit engulfs my skin
With sensuous longings, such rapport within.

For this is not only a dream, it is reality astounding
For your beauty is such, my love is abounding,
Like a flower in the springtime, as a star in the sky
Our love will last forever for we were meant, you
and I.

A Real Cool Chick

I love her like no other woman
She is a real cool chick,
She has the brains of a scientist
And she knows how to make a guy tick.

Very attractive and body beautiful
Her sensuality drives me insane,
She is very passionate when making love
Her caress so soft as a gentle rain.

She gently touches me with butterfly kisses
She fills up my senses like a perfumed flower,
The beauty of her hypnotic blue eyes
With her heaving breasts and sexual power.

She gives to this heart of mine so much happiness
A divine beauty in body, mind and soul,
Like a spring day she is full of freshness and life
I'll love her forever until the water runs dry in
life's bowl.

Angel Face

Her angelic looks, her sweet smile
Mean the world to me,
She's as heavenly as the clouds above
As wonderful as the deep blue sea.

She is a rose amongst roses
Her skin a soft delicate white,
So smooth and beautiful
So sensuous, delicious and light.

She is a queen of delicate beauty
She doesn't need to utter a sound,
Her deep ocean eyes talk to me
Her radiance glows all around.

She has calm poise and beauty
She is a love I want to embrace,
I have never come across any woman
Before with such natural beauty in her face.

At a Glance

All I have to give is love
And love you all I can,
Love is the richest feeling
Between a woman and a man.

Such beauty is never foretold
It can happen at a glance,
When we stop to smell the flowers
Love can overpower us by chance.

Like a flowing river it becomes clear
The romance and the passionate kisses,
The looks across a crowded room
Dreams of the future and wishes.

Autumn, winter, spring and summer
Love brings happiness and elation,
Like the flowers in a beautiful garden
Love is a wonderful creation.

It fills the senses, warms the heart with joy
There is nothing that can compare,
For to give love and to create life
In harmony is a wonder to be behold and share.

At This Moment

My thoughts in the morning
As she lays naked in sleep,
I take in all her divine beauty
Her beautiful body to keep.

To feel her skin like a sculpture
Every inch sensual to the touch,
Excites me with so much passion
I want to embrace her beauty so much.

How I long at this moment
For one of her voluptuous kisses,
To look into those ocean blue eyes
And tell her these thoughts and wishes.

But for now, I will let her dream her dreams
For she has always been my dream come true,
I love her more than life or words can say
Peacefully she sleeps, as I whisper, 'I love you.'

Beautiful and Loud

Whenever I kiss your lips
It makes me feel so proud,
The love we have between us
Is so beautiful and loud.

Loud in the sense of feelings
For one another's emotion,
The compassion, the care
Life's path and river of devotion.

For without devotion to beauty
Within human creation and life,
Love would be void of all feeling
Lost within deep emotional strife.

For in giving to one another's soul
With full heart to embrace,
Is the giving of peace and happiness
To your brothers and the whole human race.

Beautiful Heart

When love comes to you
Don't turn away,
When love comes to you
Embrace it and stay.

For love is the beauty
The happiness and lease,
Love is the life force
For the calm and the peace.

Love is for romance
And passionate embrace,
Love is for sensual lips
Kisses of beauty to taste.

Her talking blue eyes
Her beautiful soft skin,
Soft heaving white breasts
Holding a beautiful heart within.

Love and you will be loved
Treat her as a princess,
Cherish and savour the moment
Handle her with respect and kindness.

And love you will find in abundance
A treasure of passionate embrace,
A love of truth and loyalty
Love that brings a smile to your face.

Blue Sky

I really love this time of year
When the sky is still blue,
The flowers are whispering in the breeze
As we walk hand in hand, me and you.

I want it to be like this forever
It seems too good to be true,
Please don't let me wake up
We have so much happiness, me and you.

I'm so high on love's emotion
I feel as if I could fly,
Fly right up to the puffy white clouds
And touch the beautiful blue sky.

Just like an angel with wings as pure as snow
So, refreshing as a mountain spring,
Oh what a wonderful feeling this is
I'm so happy I want to dance and sing.

We walk through the park of beauty
Colours dazzle and sway,
With so much love in the air
These moments are in my memory to stay.

On the park bench we kissed with a passion
As the birds sang a tune of love,
The yellow sun shone down on us
It was a time from heaven above.

So, I really love it when the sky is blue
It reminds me of us you know,
When we as two lovers walked hand in hand
Through this park of love many years ago.

Breathtaking Happiness

I want to hold you in my arms
And love you until I weep,
Because this feeling I have
Overflows from my heart, that's why.

A feeling of such passion
I can't explain this elation inside,
I'm crazy for you, crazy for you
You refresh me like an incoming tide.

Your breathtaking beauty
Your voluptuous sweet kisses,
The bouquet of your skin
Are all my romantic wishes.

Your sea blue, come to bed eyes
That sensual seductive gaze,
Fills up my senses to overflowing
You have such passionate ways.

Just to touch your angelic skin
So divine and so pure,
Is to know love and beauty
And lovemaking like never before.

This love is everlasting
I embrace your love with all my heart,
Because love is happiness
And that's what you have given me from
the start.

Cherry Red

They are ripe and red and juicy
As I pick one, they remind me of you,
Voluptuous like your cherry red lips
I sit under the tree and devour two.

They remind me of your beauty
Your sensuality, your love,
So perfect in texture and skin
Created from heaven above.

I desire them as I desire your warmth
For to kiss them reminds me of our romance,
I kiss them as I would kiss you gently
I fell in love with them at the first glance.

They remind me every day of our love and passion
They are ripe, red and juicy, a beauty to behold,
In my mind's eye I can see them always
Dancing merrily in the breeze like a bar of red
gold.

Cherry Red Lips

As I held her in my arms
Her radiance held my heart,
Like the sparkling stars above
Her beauty had won from the start.

As I kissed her cherry red lips
They tasted of strawberries and cream,
The softness of her angelic breasts
I looked into her eyes and there I saw a
dream.

A dream full of rainbows, colours all
aglow
Where angels sang a song of love so pure,
I was mesmerised at the feeling of calm
The beauty, the passion, I just hoped there
was no cure.

This angelic beauty before me smiled
And said do you want more?
Are you happy? I love you so much
There is no cure for real love, what are
you waiting for?

I loved her more than life itself
And on this summer night,
The passion flowed endlessly
Until the morning light.

Complete Devotion

Let love be ours eternally
Love is all I have to give,
The passion I feel in my soul
Love is sweet, love is to live.

To give of one's whole self
Is to declare complete devotion,
This I find, my beautiful one
Is true love not just a notion?

It is romance, it breathes fresh air
Rose petals, passion and kisses,
Wonderful music and great joy
Feelings of love, dreams and wishes.

For love can be ours eternally
The beauty, the rainbows of life,
If we believe in each other
We can climb mountains without strife.

If this is our destiny, my beautiful one
Let this passion and love create,
A wonderful symphony of peace everlasting
One that will always look for love, not hate

Congratulations

The allure of your beauty
Those sexy come to bed eyes,
Leave me trembling my darling
You are like a statuette prize.

And I am the receiver
Of your love and affection,
And as I walk up to collect you
This is romantic perfection.

I embrace and I kiss you
There is such emotional elation,
The love that I feel in my heart
The crowd cheer in congratulation.

For you are my sunshine girl
Fun and beauty to embrace,
And I thank God in heaven
For your loving nature and grace.

Count The Stars for Fun

I want to kiss you all night long
These feelings are so strong,
I want to hold you forever
I know these feelings can't be wrong.

I feel passions loving hold
For such is your beautiful embrace,
Your mesmerising eyes of ocean blue
And your cherry red lips to taste.

For if this is love and being content
Then I will give you my heart,
To hold forever more in your arms
I have loved you right from the start.

Our love will be so romantic, my sweet one
We'll go boating and have picnics in the
sun,
We'll make passionate love under the
moonlight
Then lie on the riverbank and count the
stars for fun.

Dancing Blue Eyes

I'm going to love you forever
Until the stars go out with the moon,
I'm going to love you forever
On passionate nights with a tune.

A tune of love and of dancing
Every night will be one of romancing,
Of love and music and tender kisses
Under the lights your beauty is so enchanting

Your loveliness and smile excite me
You are a dream of a dreamers embrace,
You are the bell of the ball my darling
You are the most beautiful woman in this place.

They danced the whole evening forever
He danced into her sea blue eyes,
He touched her cherry red lips in a whisper
They kissed passionately amongst sighs.

There were smiles all across the dance floor,
As they swayed to the music and dance,
Young love, and all it means to them
Spending an evening of love and romance.

Deep Love Within

She looked so wonderful as she stood behind me
In the mirror and wrapped her arms around my
waist,
And hugged me so tight and whispered love into
my ear
Passionately I took in the aroma of her perfume
and taste.

I carried her up the staircase in all her radiance
and beauty
I felt love that only love can feel in this moment
of elation,
Happiness overcame me in this love-filled heart of
mine
For God in all his love had given me an angel of
divine creation.

She touched every part of my heart, life and soul
And as I kissed her gently and began to stroke her
beautiful skin,
I began to realise what a beautiful human being
she was
As I looked into her blue eyes and saw the deep
love within.

The love I felt was sent from heaven, this I can convey
I will never forget the most beautiful love making of all,
The elation, the movement, passion, we went to the ball
So, if you believe in true love look in the mirror in the hall.

Divine Beauty

When I kissed you
Our hearts became one,
Love flowed over us
Like the warmth of the sun.

The passion, the depth
Of this emotional elation,
Left me breathless with joy
To kiss such lips of divine creation.

Your soft skin, so smooth to the touch
Your angelic breasts as white as the dove,
Beauty so radiant, eyes like the stars
You really are an angel sent from above.

I have loved beauty all my life
You are the happiness of a dream come true,
Shall we get wed in the fall my darling
I will love you with all my heart I promise
you.

Divine Love

To touch you
To feel, the love we have
Between us is divine
You are of such goodness.

You bring me such warmth
I cannot express this enough,
In our time together
You have made my life blissful.

And so rich in every way
I never knew love
Could be so beautiful,
Bringing so much happiness.

To one's heart and soul
My ever-grateful heart
Will always embrace,
The day you came into my life.

I give thanks to the Lord
For your love and beauty,
Your kindness and patience
In understanding my position.

A position I must say
Was out of my hands at the time,
And you, my beautiful one
Took me on with open arms.

With your compassionate soul
You listened to me and bathed
My wounds with your kindness
And precious understanding.

I had never known such love
From one human being to another,
You gave me back my life
My reason to want to live again.

You gave me your love
You have shown me real love,
Something that I had never known
And for that I shall always be grateful.

Dreamer

When floating through
My dreams at night,
I kiss your precious face.
Soft, gentle and radiant
Your smile so sweet
I love this dreamy place.

For within this dream
Your beauty captivates me,
We have a love so pure
My beating heart feels
So full of passion, my sweet one,
I want to stay dreamy forever more.

I kiss your voluptuous lips
I embrace your heart and soul,
I touch your beauty, my divine one
The love in my heart overflows.
For you are my love's dream
Love's longing, imagination and fun.

Whether dreaming or not my sweet one
You are so alluring and beautiful,
You fill up my senses with love
Like a wonderful glorious spring day,
A heart could not help but love you
In dreams on a starry romantic night.

Elation of Love

I look into her sparkling eyes
They speak to me in ocean blue,
I see the love in them so beautiful
They fill my passionate senses too.

We love and give to each other
Feelings of sensual emotion,
We talk to the midnight stars
Kissing passionately with devotion.

Our love is magical, so special
When we touch or embrace,
Her beauty is radiant and glowing
Her skin is soft and gentle to taste.

Lovemaking is sheer joy and pleasure
A paradise of sensual, sexual sensation,
This woman gives so much to me
In love beauty and pure creation.

Embrace It

This Christmas I want you
To feel the love I have for you,
I want you to feel the passion
Within my heart and soul.
I want you to embrace it
As if you had never loved before.
Enjoying every minute of elation
Feeling the warmth from within,
The tender kisses on your sweet lips
As I run my, fingertips through your hair.
The swell of your divine breasts
As my hands caress their beauty,
As we take in the atmosphere
And gaze into each other's eyes
We feel the joy and ecstasy
Of each other's sensual physical love.
Hope for the future everlasting
At this Christmas time we give thanks
For the love and beauty found
In our hearts and souls for each other,
For the rainbow of life's colours
For the stars in the night sky
For that baby in a manger
Who died so we might live you and I!

Essence of Life

As long as we have love
We can give love
For true love is pure.

Its purity is a treasure
Of beauty and elation
That comes from the heart.

A human emotion
With so much appeal
Like the warmth of the sun.

Sharing feelings of joy
Happiness, smiles and fun
Show love to everyone.

For peace and love
Is the essence of life
And perfect bliss.

The romance and passion
To touch, to feel, to need
To embrace love.

To create, to sow a seed
Of beauty, to create life
From the gift of love.

The elation and the kisses
The sheer embrace
Of a child's birth.

There is nothing to compare
To share with those, you love
So, give love and show you care.

It makes the world a better place
It brings smiles to every face
Peace calm and joy to the human race.

Evermore

Everything you do for me
And everything you say,
Makes me feel brand new
Really makes my day.

Some days when I'm feeling blue
I only have to think of you,
And it makes me smile
It makes me so happy too.

It gives me joy within my heart
I can see your beautiful face,
I weep because I love you
I can see you in that beautiful lace.

We're Anthony and Cleopatra, you and I
We're the icing on the cake,
We're the richness full of passion
I'll never love another, make no mistake.

Everything

The love you give me
Makes my heart sing,
Your beauty a gift
For you're everything.

An angel of such passion
An elixir of honey kisses,
A romantic rose
All my dreams and wishes.

Without your love
My world would end,
In tattered pieces, my beauty
So I thank you for so much love.

Feelings

If someone tells you that they love you
If someone tells you that they care,
Do you weep with the emotion of it all
Or do you just stop and stand and stare.

Maybe no-one ever told you before
That's why you can't take it in,
That's why you begin to weep with emotion
Because you have always been used to lies and
sin.

They didn't know that, it was just a natural
reaction
They were brought up with love not deceit,
Through your tears, you tell them more
And you learn that true love cannot be beat.

You don't want them to feel sorry for your life of
pain
You want their love to be patient not demanding,
Love for you takes time you must feel secure
Warmth and tenderness, needs to be given with
understanding.

For true love can mean joy and life's happiness
A feeling maybe you have never experienced before,
So, it's better to get it right from the start than to live a
life of misery, pain and more.

Feelings Within

Darling I will love you forever
You are so refreshing to touch,
A picture so beautiful and divine
You fill my heart I love you so much.

We can't waste a moment
You make my heart overflow,
With so much love for you
Our romance can only grow.

Grow stronger, my sweet one
Under this heavenly starlight,
On this passionate evening
I just want to embrace you all night.

To kiss your voluptuous lips
Fill up my senses with your bouquet,
Stare into your ocean blue eyes,
That talk to me in a very special way.

To feel the warmth of your body
To touch the purity of your soft skin
To feel the love and warmth together
The sensual body feelings within.

To love you under the stars forever
With all my heart and soul,
Thank you, my angel, my divine one
For you have made my life quite whole.

Fly to The Moon

Kiss me, hold me
With your love so divine,
Embrace me with your charms
Tell me that you will always be mine.

Speak to me in those sexy tones
Send a shiver through my skin,
Fill my senses up with seductive play
Entice me with that alluring sexy grin.

As we search inside each other's eyes
Fly me to the moon, so we can play
Amongst the stars in sensual mood
With passionate kisses at the end of each day.

For Evermore

My body aches for your love
I ache for your voluptuous lips,
Your beautiful seductive body
Your alluring, silky smooth hips.

Passion is you with your come to bed eyes
Your divine angel breasts, tenderness to
caress,
To embrace your beauty, to cherish your skin
At this passion-filled time, simply the best.

This is the love it goes without saying
The magic, the romance, the seductive allure,
This is life, the joy, the elation of giving
The beauty of the senses and more.

To smell the roses, the elixir of living
The divine angelic body of a woman's
embrace,
To touch, to feel the heat and love
Of a woman's beauty is heaven to taste.

The sheer passion, the emotion is bliss
If love in a look from eyes divine,
Brought all your wishes to the fore,
Then my wish would always be
To smell the love and roses for evermore.

Full of Remorse

Love me like I love you
Don't let the tear drops fall,
Like summer rain
Or winters numbing call.

Let love refresh us with some calm
Embracing warmth of sun,
Let's not argue my sweet one
Over what has been said and done.

For is it not said that love can conquer
We have loved and conquered life's strife,
Climbed mountains that were insurmountable
We had love and strength my dear wife.

Why have we, succumbed to such weakness
To give in to this path of self and woe,
Is it that we have taken each other, for granted
Through the years, I suppose this must be so.

We have both said things on reflection
That were most hurtful and full of remorse,
But of course, we can forgive and forget
That's what love and marriage is about of
course.

Love is about these sometimes, petty things
But this time, it just got out of hand,
My love for you is forever my darling
Marriages fall foul of this all over the land.

He held her in a warm embrace
And kissed her beauty like the sun,
They both knew true love could never fade
She was the flower of his life, the only one.

Genuine Love

To love, and to be loved is heaven
For genuine love is sure.
Like the love of a child,
Beautiful as a snowdrop and pure.
Love each other in the sunshine,
Love each other in the rain.
Laugh with love in your heart and soul,
For you have so much to gain.
Laugh with love in your heart
For there can be no greater elation.
It's as fresh as a flower in the morning dew,
Love that brings colours of rainbows hue.
To love is to touch God's creation in life,
In peace and calm without the strife.

Gift of Your Smile

When I receive the gift of your smile
The world is a much brighter place,
It creates love and warmth all around me,
Your beauty and kisses are wonderful to taste.

Love is in the air on this passionate spring day
Romance in the sunshine of love's sweet bouquet,
To touch you, to look into your azure blue eyes
Your skin like the petals of blossom so soft as we
lay.

By the river of life in all its fresh glorious wonder
The colours the beauty of a new spring day,
I embrace it all as I embrace your beauty my sweet
My love overflows and may it always be this way.

Give to One Another

Love decides most everything
It makes the world a better place,
It makes you smile and laugh
Yes, love gives you a cheerful face.

It makes you happy in your work
It makes you happy at play,
Wherever you go in life
Love makes for a happy day.

Sometimes we weep with happiness
Because of the things we love,
The beauty in a child's face
For which we thank the Lord above.

We all need love to help us
To conquer our fears and trials,
We all need that cuddle of reassurance
Even though it may be across the miles.

Love can do most anything in life
For relationships young and old,
Keep them warm in the knowledge
That they are loved and not out in the cold.

For life is so precious, the beauty overflows
The baby lamb in spring, the flowers of all
hues,
So give to one another so that beauty grows
God gave us all this with love to write in
our muse.

Golden Touch

I love to hear you laugh, I said
It puts a sparkle in your eye,
It's so infectious it makes me happy
I love you so much I almost want to cry.

To weep some happy tears of love
Because you have given me so much,
Because you're so wonderful and daft
You just have that golden touch.

You're intelligent, beautiful and kind
I want to hug you, twenty, four seven,
You make me feel so sublime
You're like an angel sent from heaven.

They chatted into the daylight
Until the romantic stars went to bed,
And as she fell asleep in his arms
He whispered I love you,
This time next year we'll be wed.

Greatest of All Emotions

I love you from the depths of my soul
Every moment, minute of every day,
This love this passion embraces my heart
It possesses my strength, what more can I say.

For love is the greatest of all emotions
It is a beauty of power to hold and wish,
To embrace with all tenderness in life
To treat gentle and caress like a first kiss.

To feel beauty in all of its creation
Love makes for such emotional joy,
A dream of a lover's, wish so true
Between the innocence of girl and boy.

For there is no other feeling like it
The stare, the touch of the soft skin,
Within the beauty of pure love
There beats a heart of happiness within.

Hand in Hand

It was a beautiful evening
As we walked through the sand,
We were passionate about each other
We walked barefoot, hand in hand.

The silver stars shone above us
The ocean whispered at our feet,
As we stopped to sit on the sand
This romantic setting was complete.

It filled up our senses as we embraced
Our sensual juices coming to the fore,
As we touched and kissed passionately
We made beautiful love on this midnight shore.

It was an evening of utter elation
And as we lay, in each other's arms,
We talked late into the night
About our future and mother natures charms.

About the love and the beauty around us
How creation brought about love,
Bringing happiness to us both
Under the planets and stars above.

Harmony's Embrace

Beautiful thoughts under a blue sky
Looking into love's blue eyes,
A divine angel lies by my side
Sensual kissing beneath summer skies.

The blossom tree of romantic petals
Floats softly in a whispering breeze,
Like a pillow of feathers floating
All around from the paradise of trees.

This love, this passion, this warm
Tender loving embrace,
Fills up my senses to overflowing
As I feel her soft skin in every place.

Her angelic white breasts to touch
Are so heavenly beautiful and pure,
As I caress and kiss this angel before me
I know this is love I have never felt before.

For I feel such elation and joy in my heart
We're joined together in harmony's embrace,
Two people under the summer skies
Who found love in such an, idyllic place.

Here In My Heart

I hold a place here in my heart
And that place is for you,
Full of warmth and love
With a pure happiness too.

It is for your beauty
Your giving, kindness and truth,
It is because you're an angel
For never being unkind or uncouth.

You are the smiles of my existence
My undoubted emotional being,
You are my eyes of such beauty
The sun, the moon, the stars for seeing.

You're my rock of salvation
The ocean calm and serene,
The very foundation of my peace
Built on trust, love and a dream.

For such loyalty and compassion
Can only come from a loving heart,
One that can see the beauty in you
A beautiful friend right from the start.

Hold Me All Night

Hold me all night long baby
Embrace me with your love,
As I gaze into her blue eyes
I see a divine angel from above.

With a smile so warm and beautiful
I kiss her lips of voluptuous ruby red,
I caress her pure white breasts
The passion begins in her rose petal bed.

I caress, her beauty, it feels so good
Her soft baby skin tastes so sweet,
Making love is so wonderful
Gentle love brings us to elation complete.

As we lay, we kiss, and we touch
The picture is one of love and romance,
As we gaze at the stars through the skylight
The stars had not shone on us by chance.

Hold On To Me

Hold onto me baby
I'll never let you go,
Just sway to the rhythm
Of my heartbeat just so.

Can you; hear it beating
The love I feel for you,
Can you, hear the music
It's playing right on cue.

Cause when we touch
I feel happy inside,
This romantic evening
These feelings I can't hide.

This passion, this love
Your sweet lips I kiss,
Fill my senses to overflowing
For you are my dream my wish.

You are the beauty of all stars
And as I gaze into your blue eyes,
I see a rainbow of happiness
A love so deep from heavenly skies.

For you are my perfect angel
My breath my life my soul,
You are my calm on stormy water
You my love are my life's bowl.

I Love You, I Love You, I Love You

I have never had such a feeling
Do you feel it too?
I feel so warm inside
I want to weep with happiness
Because I love you so much,
Let me put my arms around you
I want to hold you forever
When I'm with you
This feeling just gets better and better
I love you with every part of my being
With every bit of my heart and soul
I want to kiss every inch
Of your sweet passionate beautiful body,
I never want to let you go.
I have dreamt about this moment
And falling in love it's so wonderful
I never knew what love was until we met
I have heard other couples talk about love
And now I know for myself,
You are the best thing that's ever happened
to me
And I love you, I love you, I LOVE YOU

You have given me something more precious
than gold
You have given me love and made my life so
happy
I want to shout it out to the world how much
I love you
I love, you, I love you, I LOVE YOU!

I Love Thee More

I love you more than life itself
I love you, like a brand, new day,
I love you like the shining stars
I will always love you, this I pray.

For you are the precious jewel
Whose beauty I love to embrace,
Whose sensual lips I love to kiss
To touch and caress your pretty face.

To look into your eyes of passion
To see the deep love within,
To feel your heartbeat next to mine
I know beautiful lovemaking is about to begin.

We touch, kiss and explore each other
Her heavenly breasts are pure and white,
Our bodies aroused by the feel and touch
Her beauty is that of an angelic delight.

Such beauty to caress and hold,
Such innocence and purity, simply divine,
To love, to be a friend forever more
Like a baby lamb, in glorious springtime.

I'll Be Gentle

What do you want from me baby?
What is it you want me to do?
What is it you want from me baby?
I'll be gentle, I promise you.

I'll take your tender heart and hold it
Love you and keep you warm,
Love you forever my darling
Keep you safe from any storm.

Love me like I love you
Hold me oh so close,
Let me feel your heartbeat
Your lips that are the most.

Your kisses are like wine
Feel the romance,
Hold me closer darling
Enjoy this moment and dance.

Dance with the stars my beauty
Feel the wonder of this place,
Let's stay here forever
Two hearts in a loving embrace.

In The Warm Night Air

We gazed into each other's eyes
The moonlight kissed her golden hair,
The night was warm with romance
Passionately we kissed in the warm night air.

Her skin so soft, like that of a newborn child
Like summer roses, her bouquet so sweet,
Her cherry red lips tasted of honey
Her beauty so divine, to embrace complete.

Her heaving breasts were as pure as snow
She looked like an angel on this warm night,
She filled my senses to overflowing
We made love underneath the moonlight.

I have never felt such love and elation
As our bodies entwined in passionate embrace,
This love, this beauty, this wonderful feeling
Enraptured my heart and soul in this place.

So precious was this moment in time
I guess you know I have a smile on my face,
I will recall and remember this love always
Because she had both beauty, class and not haste.

In This Moment

On a starlit night on the shore
As I gaze into your big brown eyes,
I realise how stunningly beautiful you are
As we gently kiss under the night skies.

This moment is to treasure forever
With love that is so magical and pure,
In this moment, in this hour together
We discover the meaning of true love for sure.

For without love in these brief encounters
Love would have no meaning or sense at all,
Just to touch your beautiful body with a kiss
Sends my heart racing like the oceans' call.

For life and reality wouldn't exist without you
You are my oxygen in life's gateway of love,
My beauty in a garden of perfumed flowers
To have this time together is a blessing from
above.

Just a Fool

I don't know where she's living
I don't know where she goes,
I only know that we are not together
We stopped, why, goodness knows.

I watched her the other night
She was on some other guys arm,
They went into a nightclub
Smiling sweetly at each other, full of charm.

I don't know where I went wrong
She's with another guy,
I suppose he'll buy her diamond rings
I wanted her and I to have another try.

But now she's gone and messed up
Although she's trying to act cool,
I know she'll blow this other guy away
And I know I'll take her back like a fool.

Cause I can't live without her
She does things for me man,
I know I'm crazy out of my head
I just got to love her the best way I can.

Just Love Me

Don't try to understand me
Just love me, for who I am,
Don't try to understand me
Just cuddle me like a lamb.

Hold me all through the night
And never ever let me go,
Just love me for who I am
You're such a loving soul.

Don't try to understand me
Just give me your love to keep,
And I will repay you forever
For ours is the world to reap.

To reap and to be fulfilled
In knowing this our love will grow,
To hear the patter of tiny feet
Love, children and happiness all in a row.

Just Tell Me She Is No Dream

Within me lies a love
A pure angelic sight,
With feelings from the heart
With a love that is so bright.

She is a beauty of such desire
Her radiance as pure as snow,
Her passion is delightful
Our love can only grow.

She fills my senses with happiness
Love grows with each joyful kiss,
I cannot but love her tenderness
For she is my life's wish.

I could not wish for more love
My heart aches when she is missing,
For I couldn't last a day
Without her embrace and kissing.

Her eyes are hypnotic
Her body so beautiful and pure,
I will love her forever
And I hope there is no cure.

I have never known such love
Please tell me this is not a dream,
Please let this be reality
And that love will always be the theme.

Just To Hold You

I love you with all good faith
I love you with my beating heart,
Your beauty is mesmerising
Your blue eyes hypnotised me from the start.

You fill up my senses to overflowing
There is no place I would rather be,
I want to embrace your beauty forever
We were meant for this moment you and me.

You fulfil me like a beautiful rainbow
everlasting
Like the colours you make my life so bright,
The joy happiness and elation you bring me
Makes me dance and sing with utter delight.

The passion and love that I feel just to hold you
For in the entire world I can't explain,
Just to kiss your cherry red lips
And feel your body next to mine drives me
insane.

For you are the rose of all roses simply divine
You have made my wishes come true,
You have made my life so happy and complete
Yes, said Angela, I feel the same way about you.

Just You and I

Baby I love you because you understand me
I love you because you're you,
I love you because you make me happy
And you never make me feel blue.

You're like the beauty of a sunshine day
That shines on your angel face,
The divinity that is sent from heaven
You complete the happiness around this place.

The colour of a budding flower to the eye
Such graceful beauty so soft and sweet,
And as I touch and kiss your cherry red lips
I feel the love and warmth between us so
complete.

Your body has a bouquet, of sweet, smelling
roses
My romantic, passionate senses are full, with
elation,
With every breath let us savour this moment
I love you my divine one for you are a beautiful
creation.

Kiss Me On The Cheek

Come kiss me on the cheek my love
Don't let this moment pass by,
Let me feel your hot breath upon my skin
Your beauty is like pure diamonds in the sky.

I love your flowing locks like the golden sun
I love your heaving breasts so pure,
I adore your ocean blue eyes
Every day that passes, I love you even more.

Your skin feels so soft and tender to touch
On this warm evening your lips a delight,
You just fill my senses up to overflowing
On this romantic evening we two are just right.

For this night my divine angel of beauty
Is so perfect in God's garden of love,
In my heart and soul, I couldn't wish for more
As I sit here and caress your beauty,
My heart flows with thanks to the Lord above.

Kiss Me In The Rain

Love me like I love you
Kiss me in the rain,
Let us share the rainbows
Of life let happiness be our gain.

Travel the road of sunshine
Blue skies to embrace,
The beauty of the stars at night
The romance of mother earth's face.

Enjoy the freedom to explore
The love in this romantic place,
To breath to fill up our senses
To enjoy each other's taste.

The sensual moment of this time
As I kiss you my sweet one,
I am reminded of cherries
So voluptuous and fun.

Your breasts look divine
In this romantic moonlight,
Your eyes I simply adore
Your beauty is a glorious sight.

The love I feel in this atmosphere,
I don't want this night to end,
You fill me with joy and elation
For you are my lover and best friend.

I have no other way to express
My adoration, I love you so very much,
Your beauty fills up my heart and soul
You are my life and emotional crutch.

Kisses of Beauty

I'm going to love you forever
Until the stars no longer shine,
Love you my beautiful princess
With this beating heart of mine.

For you are my sunshine
My rainbow of dreams,
My bowl of strawberries
And delicious ice creams.

Passion, romance, radiance
Your come to bed eyes,
You give to me your soul
Like the brilliant blue skies.

Your soft skin to touch
So tender and mild,
Vivacious energy
That sends me sensually wild.

You're like a fresh spring flower
I just want your beauty to hold,
Because to me my wonderful darling
Your charm and beauty will always be gold.

Kisses of Love

You are my little sunshine girl
I love you from head to toe,
I couldn't imagine life without you
Your beauty embraces me so.

Your sunshine fills me with joy
Those come to bed eyes so blue,
You're like an angel soft and pure
I love you sunshine for being you.

You make me happy and fulfilled
You're the music of my soul,
My dreams and wishes my elation
My cream in life's beautiful bowl.

You are the colours of my rainbow
All wrapped up with a bow of fun,
So delicious to taste like chocolates
With kisses of pure love in everyone.

Kisses of Love and Life

When love comes along
Keep it for all time,
When love comes along
Write a love poem in rhyme.

One that you can share
In the nostalgic years of age,
To remember passionate kisses
So tender as you turn each page.

The pages of life and love
Moonlit walks on the shore,
The romantic wedded bliss
Happiness, love and more.

The patter of tiny feet
How they grew so very quick,
How you loved them and nursed them
Cuddled them when they were sick.

How the time has flown by
But written and recorded right here,
Beautiful memories to browse
For your grandchildren to admire, my dear.

Like a Spring day

Hold my heart if you love me
Let me embrace your beauty in my arms,
Let me look into those sea-blue eyes
And kiss your ravishing lips and charms.

For you are to me like a spring day
So refreshing colourful and bright,
A new dawn in my life has begun
Of joy, happiness and delight.

A passionate time of devotion
For love and beauty are not just words,
They are wonderful tender emotions
That can make your heart sing like the birds.

Love can make you kind of dreamy
Love can make you stop and smell the flowers,
Listen to a classical orchestra playing
As you kiss beneath the romantic moonlight for
hours.

Love is a heart overflowing with depth
With feelings you sometimes cannot explain,
But you know you want them to last forever
Because love brings you so much happiness and
gain.

Like a Thousand Rainbows

Kisses of your beautiful lips
Romantic wishes and dreams,
I take sips of your loveliness
I have loved you forever it seems.

Under heaven's passionate starry skies
In the moonlight your radiance flows,
My heart and soul will forever be yours
For with every passing year your beauty grows.

For you are the rose of all roses
Your soft gentle touch I simply adore,
To hold you in my embrace for just a moment
Your blue eyes speak of love so pure.

You are an angel so divine in passion
A diamond that sparkles so bright,
You bring me happiness like a thousand
rainbows
Like the beautiful stars glittering at night.

For the world I wouldn't change you my sweet
I have loved you since the beginning of creation,
Since your beauty and smell of blossom
fragrance
Caught me in its spell under the blossom tree of
pure elation.

The romance and the passion on this beautiful
evening
I must confess your beauty is of an angel I just
want more,
My heart and soul are yearning for it to never
end
My angel, for I love you so much I hope there's
no cure.

When love brings so much joy and excitement to
one's life
And the sun, moon and stars all agree to be a
part of that love,
And all your wishes and dreams and everything
you ever wanted
It must be all part of God's plan for us up in
heaven above.

Love's Bowl

Our lips touched, the night was full of magic
The moon was high on the cloud,
Passion was in the warm night air
In the silence her beauty sang out loud.

Her skin was like that of a newborn baby
Her mesmerising eyes were ocean blue,
I fell in love with her from that moment
She took me to the moon and stars too.

She sang to me with every part of her being
She had love in every ounce of her soul,
This was true love and being content
We had taken and loved from life's bowl.

She knew how to love with a passion
She was a seed of intense love and creation,
In all of my life I never knew a woman
That could bring me such beautiful elation.

We lay under the moon and starlit kisses
We thrilled to the sounds of the night,
And as we lay holding hands with whispers
We both knew that love and the future were
bright.

Love So Deep

Quench my heart and soul
With your love so deep,
Embrace me with such feeling
So as to make me weep.

My darling with such happiness
With tears of so much elation,
This with your beauty caress me
Hold me like the rainbow of creation.

For you fill me up to overflowing
With your sensual red lip kisses,
Your passionate soft arousing touch
You fulfil my dreams and wishes.

Your adoring hypnotic blue eyes
So romantic, like a starlit night,
Just send me crazy with love for you
Your alluring beauty is a wonderful sight.

This love, this passion overwhelms me
You bring to my life so much fun,
I kiss the heavens for an angel
And I was sent a passionate and caring one.

Loving Sunshine Gal

Give me a gal that can
Show me true love
Even though she's cheeky
Through her smiles,
One that has beauty to waste
Like a sunshine day
That gets me over
The hurdles and stiles.

And I'll give that gal
So much loving
Fun and laughter,
Everyday to embrace
She'll think she's
Living in paradise
With joy and happiness
Always on her pretty face.

I would buy her ribbons
To go with her beautiful
Blue eyes and blond curls,
Love her with lots of passion
Treat her like royalty,
Wine and dine her like a queen
Respect her clothes and fashion.

We would smell the roses
Embrace life with joy in our hearts
'Cause life is for living my friends,
Compassion and caring are all a part
Of the giving of love and the music,
The life and the love and the sharing,
And now I've found my sunshine girl
It's all about the embrace of beauty and
caring.

Mesmerising Blue

When love walks in the room
It sends a shiver down your spine,
It stops you in your tracks
The beauty of love is hard to define.

That special moment, that look
Gets your heart beating fast,
As you endeavour to speak
The spell has been cast.

The beauty, before you, smiles
You get tongue-tied for a while,
Her ocean-blue eyes never leave you
They are mesmerising, she has got style.

She has class and breeding
Cambridge bred with degrees to the ceiling,
Romantic and passionate about life
She loves nature, which to you is appealing.

You ask her out, she smiles over dinner
You have the most beautiful conversation,
You tell her you are a writer and poet
She says poets are good reading for the nation.

She is so charming and intelligent
I fell in love and I'm glad love came to call,
Yes, it was fate and I have to thank
Those beautiful blue eyes that started it all.

Moment to Treasure

It was a beautiful evening
We danced by the shore,
In her flowing red dress
She looked radiant and more.

She was a princess of beauty
Her love of music danced in her eyes,
As the orchestra played a love song
To the whisper, of the oceans, cries.

Cries to the romance and passion
Of a beautiful, couples, pleasure,
Under the moonlight of elation
They embraced this moment to treasure.

To treasure the happiness of true love
To feel the touch of life's bouquet,
The richness and the wisdom
Of each other's happiness each day.

They sat by the golden sands, everlasting
The sparkling stars shone down with glee,
On a couple who were so much in love
As they kissed on a romantic night by the sea.

My Butterfly of Love

Come to me my sweet one
For I will bring you no tears,
You are a butterfly of love
I will protect you from any fears.

For I love you my precious one
I have watched your beauty grow,
Your radiance stands out like a flower
I have felt your warmth and glow.

I am your knight in shining armour
I am your smiling courageous Cavalier,
I am your man in the iron mask my sweetness
I am your loyal lover to protect you from fear.

For I have loved you all my life
I have loved you with a passion so great,
I have watched you flow my butterfly
My heart and soul says this must be our fate.

A fate more glorious than we could ever
imagine
For is it not so, that love conquers all,
Just say the words, my beautiful sweet one
I ask your hand my lady, can we be married in
the fall?

Arise my handsome knight she said and come
closer
She kissed him with all the love in her heart,
Love and romance blossomed under the stars
True love was forever, and they knew they
would never part.

My Heart To Yours

Do you know kid? I have loved you all my
life.
From the beginning I knew that love
Was most precious.

I have always had love in my soul.
But it took someone special to find that love
Someone special like you.

That pure love that feeling of emotion
From my heart to yours.

You brought me happiness
You brought me joy,
For the first time in my life

I knew real true love,
The kind I had never felt
This was when my life began.

My life was full of shadows,
I suppose I was still a child
Searching for compassion,

I was still floating
In an emotional sea of kelp
Behaving in an immodest way.

Seeking the shores of security
My confidence being a fake
To show the world I could make it.

But faking it was a failure
People recognised my mask,
I wasn't fooling anyone

As my tears of childhood
Drowned me like a lake,
I searched my mind for answers.

I prayed that love
Would find me one day,
In the darkness of my life

I prayed that one day
I would find love,
Someone to care for real.

I found that real love
In you my angel
You brought it out of me.

The love and compassion
Of childhood years
Flowed like a river.

Of utter joy and elation
I have found someone
Who loves and cares,

And whose beauty
Will fill my world forever,
You brought out my creative role.

So, here's looking at you kid
I love you with all my heart and soul.

My Rainbow

Let me love you
Your beauty I love to embrace,
Let me see that wonderful smile
Let me kiss that beautiful face.

For you bring to this heart such happiness
This soul cannot hide emotions of love,
You are the flower of all my dreams
All my rainbows in the sky above.

You are the stars that caress me at night
You are a picture of love peace and charm,
The passion, romance and the moonlight
You are the beauty that makes me feel calm.

You fill up my senses to overflowing
Like perfumed flowers in a garden of peace,
I feel such joy in your company
May this love and friendship never cease.

Non Existent

It's a pleasure for me
To love you,
Because I didn't
Always feel this way.

I never had love
As a child,
They always
Pushed me away.

I have no doubt
They did love me,
But it wasn't
In the family rule.

It took me twenty years
To love someone,
I found it in her heart
And eyes of ocean blue.

The first time she told me
That she loved me,
I said you love me
You mean it, you really do.

I had never had
The feeling of love before,
She taught me what love was
That love was to care.

She taught me that compassion
Was better than aggression or fear,
In my case love was replaced
With aggravation violence and beer.

That's why I never knew love
Because violence got in the way.
Kisses and cuddles were not
A part of my childhood life.

It was never a part of the equation
The word love was never spoken,
I have found out how beautiful
Love is and it has brought me happiness
Like I have never known.

Not a Fantasy or a Dream

Our love is like the colours
Of natures picture show,
So very beautiful and romantic
Like a warm sunshine glow.

So blissful and serene
Not a fantasy or a dream,
Not an illusion or a hope
This love of ours is the cream.

The cream on a Birthday cake
Engagement and wedding too,
The purity and the goodness in life
The breath of life given to me and you.

Not a Game

When love taps you on the shoulder
And your emotions bring a tear,
You can't handle the responsibility
Of real love and you feel full of fear.

Do you walk away with your conscience?
Feeling full of guilt and shame,
Or is it that you know in your heart
That he really loves you, and it's not a game

The game you've played for many years
Broken many hearts along the way,
But in your heart this time around
You really know love is here to stay.

To give you all you want in life
The rainbows of happiness and fun,
The security, roses and romance
And the beauty of love under the sun.

Nothing to Compare

All I have to give is love
And love you all I can,
Love is the richest feeling
Between a woman and a man.

Such beauty is never foretold
It can happen in a glance,
When we stop to smell the flowers
Love can overpower us by chance.

Like a flowing river it becomes clear
The romance and the passionate kisses,
The look across a crowded room
Dreams of the future and wishes.

Autumn, winter, spring and summer
Love brings happiness and elation,
Like the flowers of radiant beauty
Love is a wonderful creation.

It fills the senses and warms the heart
There is nothing that can compare,
For to give love and create life
In harmony is beauty to behold and share.

Ocean-Blue Eyes

This beauty before me
Makes me dance with elation,
She fills my heart up
For she is a divine creation.

She makes me feel good
Like the warmth of the sun,
Her smile captivates me
She is so full of zest and fun.

My love for her is eternal
Such passion I cannot conceal,
My sensual pulse races
That's how she makes me feel.

Every time I touch her soft skin
And gaze into her ocean-blue eyes,
I fall in love with her all over again
And that certain smile is no disguise

Orange Sunset

Love me like I love you
Love me in the spring,
Love me in the summer
Like the birds upon the wing.

Be gentle with me darling
I love your beauty so much,
I love you with every beat of my heart
I love your amazing caress and touch.

I love you with a passion like the stars
Like the soft woollen clouds in an azure sky,
I love you like the orange sunset
Floating over the tidal waves that cry.

Cry out at all the beauty, the radiance of life
The golden sands where love can find
elation,
The romance and the passion, the elixir so
profound
The love that fills up our senses with
creation.

Our Fate

Won't you love me?
Like you did before,
Don't ever leave me
Don't ever slam the door

Of love and fate in my face
Cause I couldn't stand the pain,
Of looking back in sorrow
My heart couldn't take the strain.

My love for you is everlasting
Like a picture painted in precious gold,
You're my treasured beauty to embrace
Please don't leave me out in the cold.

If left in the darkness of my despair
I will surely go crazy in my mind,
I would be washed out to sea
With the debris for you to find.

Give me your sweet loving
And I'll forget the sins of the past,
We were meant to be you and I
We both know our love will last.

Just think of the future my darling
We're on a slow boat of romance,
Where paradise can be simply divine
Where happiness is not just by chance.

Overwhelmed

Love takes away the hurt, the pain
Love gives elation and delight,
For if love, not be of these things
Then love itself would not be right.

Your beauty is of the brightest flower
Your hair like strands of silk,
Your soft skin is so tender to touch
And your lips taste of honey and milk.

Your eyes are of sparkling stars
Hypnotic, beautiful like the sea,
You are the jewel of my kingdom
Loving angel beauty sent to me.

The passion I feel overwhelms me
For I cannot contain it within,
I only have to look in your eyes
To see the love, we had to begin.

That love hasn't changed my angel
It grows stronger day by day,
If God in his heaven is listening
He knows that love is the way.

I go down on bended knee
My angel, my sweet, my love,
I love you more than life itself
I swear to the Lord God above.

Arise gallant knight she said
And kissed him in a fashion,
And so they galloped off into the sunset
Knowing love had won with passion.

Paradise Unknown

In silence we kissed
On the riverbank of romance,
Like the summer flowers
Her beauty made my heart dance.

Dance in the happiness of love
For this was paradise unknown,
I had never felt like this before
This all, embracing joy has grown.

The very blood of life that flowed
Through my veins in elation,
Filled me with warmth and love
For she was an angel of creation.

The colour, the beauty, the spectacle
The rainbow of natures colour glowed,
Around us in all its majestic splendour
Like her beauty, and passion it flowed.

We lay on the riverbank until moonlight
We gazed into each other's love-filled eyes,
Wishing this glorious day would never end
As we talked to the twinkling stars in the skies.

Passionate Feelings

I can feel your love
Your body heat,
Your kisses of honey
Oh, so sensual and sweet.

As we lay beside the river
The water sang a beautiful song,
Of romantic love and passion
I just wanted it to last the whole night long.

As we listened to the water flowing
As I looked into her sparkling eyes,
I saw the beauty of a rainbow
Flash across the wonder of the skies.

I felt such love and happiness in my heart
I could not help but weep upon her breast,
My heart and soul were filled with elation
So much so my deep joy I had to confess.

Love had never made me feel this way
These precious moments were mine,
I had found true love and passion
Such emotional feelings were simply divine.

As we lay beside the river
As we lay, in each, others arms,
I never knew such beautiful lovemaking
To the song of the romantic water and her
charms.

Photo of Love

Let me sing you a song
With the love that I feel,
Every time I embrace
Your photo with kisses so real.

How you fill up my senses
With your beauty and grace,
With your passion and sensuality
Your beautiful smile and taste.

Let me tell you how each kiss
Makes our hearts to be one,
Because loving you so much
Bring us warmth like the sun.

The warmth of our bodies
Your soft beautiful skin so close,
Is like heaven on earth to me
The elation I feel is the most.

For you are the rose of all roses
I miss your beautiful bouquet,
And as I look at your sparkling eyes
In this photo, these tears can only say.

I love you now as I have always loved you
This pain I feel won't go away,
So please hurry home my sweet one
This photo I will keep close to my heart
Until you come back home to stay.

Pure Sunshine

I think of spring and beauty
Like the beauty of your smile,
It makes me feel so fresh
Your personality can beguile.

The passionate colours
The passion blue of your eyes,
The cherry red of your sensual lips
You're the warm sunset in the skies.

You are the daffodil of sunshine
The love that caresses my soul,
The tenderness so sweet in my hands
The spring lamb and the baby foal.

Your freshness and colour so bright
A flower of pure love so divine,
You give to my heart such warmth
For you my love, bring me sunshine.

Radiant

The night was soft and gentle
The silence whispered like the dove,
In the romantic moonlight shadows
We kissed passionately with love.

Her heaving breasts were like blossom
So heavenly pure, delicate and white,
My pounding heart was so overcome
I confessed my undying love that night.

We lay beside the flowing waters
We lay under the starlit sky,
We made passionate and intense love
So beautiful I knew I was a lucky guy.

Her beauty is so radiant, so fresh
Her eyes hypnotic ocean blue.
She is my dream of all dreams
An angel of life and happiness too.

Romance

We danced together until midnight,
Your eyes of blue pierced my soul.
Your, very being in this atmosphere,
Your enraptured glow.
You sang to me in your silence,
Your love filled lips touched mine,
And sent me into ecstasy,
The world of sexual wine.

I loved you like no other,
You played a tune on the strings of my heart,
You brought out the best in me,
I knew we could never part.
Our love flowed like a mountain spring,
I felt as if all the world was watching us
In a kind of holy thing.

We were as two people in a picture,
For everyone to view.
Two people so in love for the good of all
mankind.
Two happy people, strong in body and in mind.
Two beings of humanity, so in touch with each
other.
Beautiful harmony, style and grace.
Movements of love with another's pace.

Romantic and tender with talking eyes,
That say I would still love you under starlit skies.
I would follow you to the end of the earth.
To touch your skin, your beauty, your worth.

For you are reality, happiness and being content.
I will love you forever in the knowledge that
ecstasy
Is the space where love can take you,
To a wonderful romantic place.

Romantic Elation

I saw you in the moonlight
Such beauty sent to earth,
From heaven's bower
From up above he gave you birth.

Such radiance my eyes have
Never beset, such an angel so divine,
With skin as pure as stars of snow
And lips that taste like the purest wine.

Let me embrace you, let me touch you
You seduce me with your hypnotic allure,
You fill up my senses with warmth and passion
I am in love with you and there is no cure.

My angel, the night is ours for passion
When I look into your eyes, they tell me so,
It is such a romantic night for love
Let's not waste this moment, love can only grow.

They made passionate love under the moonlight
To the sound of the flowing river of life,
Happiness was elation as they later walked
Hand in hand, as he asked her to be his wife.

Romantic Evening

She swam in a sea of beauty
Her looks were simply divine,
She took my breath away
Across the restaurant table
She was delectable all mine.

I loved her with a passion
Like I had never loved before,
I loved her whole being
I loved her come to bed eyes
I loved her to the very core.

As the candles flickered
It was such a romantic night
The light flickered on a love from heaven
And as we held hands across the table
I proposed, her joy was a beautiful sight.

We walked in the moonlight of love
Through the park where the roses grow,
We kissed and I picked one for her
Such beauty and class went hand in hand
I loved her with all my heart and soul.

We arrived home about two AM
I opened a bottle of champagne,
We then slid between the black satin sheets
And made passionate love all night
And celebrated for we had it all to gain.

She Is My Breath

The candlelight flickered shadows
On her features of beauty and grace,
She had a charm about her
She smiled with warmth in her face.

Her eyes sparkled full of love
Her lips were voluptuous and sweet,
As we embraced on this beautiful evening
Two romantic loving hearts began to meet.

Passion filled the air, bodies entwined
Lovemaking came like the tide of the sea,
Beautiful but gentle, satisfying elation
Exciting, full of love together you and me.

She brings me happiness, vigour and life
She is my breath my total being,
My reason to wake up with the sun
Her beauty is her smile, a joy for seeing.

She Makes My Heart Smile

I see a shining light of love
Within these walls to embrace,
As I stand and look at her beauty
She brings such radiance to this place.

She is my lover, my best friend
An angel a gift of happiness and fun,
The colour the laughter in her eyes
I feel her warmth, just like the sun.

Her talking eyes fill up my senses
Her passion fills me with elation,
Her alluring, seductive body
So soft for she is a beautiful creation.

She is my every waking moment
The very being that makes my day,
The very heart and soul of my life
I love her what more can I say.

Simply Divine

Sunlight comes softly through the window
As we lay beneath the duvet of love,
As she lay sleeping in all her beauty
She sleeps peaceful like that of a dove.

For she is as pure as a mountain spring
She smells of lavenders, sweet bouquet,
As I look at her, I kiss her gently on the cheek
For I love her more than life, what more can I say.

For she is the greatest treasure in my life
We share a love that is simply divine,
She is my laughter in times of stress
She is my sunshine like a sparkling wine.

She is there smiling when I open the door
She is my kiss and cuddle and what's even more,
She is the romance on a starlit night
She is my passion as we go through life's tour.

The light of my path always guiding my steps
And as I leave this bed of peaceful embrace,
My heart is like a rainbow of beautiful colours
I thank the Lord for this angel in all good grace.

For as long as I have breath in my body
And the sunrise and strength in my frame,
I will love her like I love the gift of life
Like the beautiful stars she is one and the same.

Stop and Smell The Flowers

There is a place I want to be
And that is in your arms,
So, I can kiss your voluptuous lips
So, I can caress your beautiful charms.

To whisper that I love you
To take you to passions Isle,
Where love is perfect bliss
And the sun shines all the while.

Where happiness is forever
Where there is always love and peace,
Where beauty is all around us
Let this wonderful love never cease.

For I love you like the blue skies above
Like the hue of the most beautiful flower,
With all my heart and soul forever
Like the time clock of life, every second, minute
and hour.

I want to touch your baby skin and hold you close
Look into those beautiful baby blue sparkling eyes,
I love you so much I weep with joy, for you are an
angel
Sent down from heaven to fulfil my dreams from
God's skies.

When I look up at the stars I stand and wonder
For on God's earth there is so much hurt and
pain,
And yet the beauty and love is abundant for all to
enjoy
If only they would stop and smell the flowers now
and again.

Sunset Over The Beach

Sunset over the beach
The sea is calm with all its charm

Sunset over the beach.

The palm trees swaying golden sands laying
Trickles of sweat beads, coconut milk
Drinking from glasses with ice-filled silk.

A foreign land where the sun shines forever
Two lovers who want to spend their lives
together.

Sunset over the beach.

Fishes swim in harmony
In a clear blue sea full of peace.

Sunset over the beach.

Their white skins turn to brown on a golden
sand
They glow in the sunset as they walk hand in
hand.

Sunset over the beach

A haven that is glorious, their wildest dreams
come true
They make passionate love beneath the stars
And swaying palm trees too.

Sunset over the beach.

As the palm trees sway above their head
Tony proposes to Pauline of whom he wants to
wed.
A dream or imagination the silver stars shine
bright
On two lovers who are so in love on a sunset
beach at night.

Sent From Heaven

Candles flicker in solitude
My mind thoughts playing games,
As shadows of a distant past,
Float merrily in the flames.
Floating music fills the air
She lies content in beanbags slumber,
While black coals burn to heat the lumber.
Her pale skin this amber light,
Flickers a tune of warmth and love,
As it flickers on a heart so pure
This angelic beauty sleeps content.
Floating music and candle soft,
I wonder what she dreams
A love so peaceful soft and sweet,
In this amber light my brain cells compete.
I send her love that hath no end,
Like a child I want to hold her tight.
I want to caress her beauty in this soft light.
For there is no greater love than what we have
And as she sleeps in her angelic pose,
I smell her perfume like that of a beautiful rose.
For she is my rose of all roses, like a beautiful
wine,
She is my love, my one and only Valentine.

Tell Her You Love Her

If love could be forever
I would spend my life with you,
For your beauty beckons
Like the cloudless sky of blue.

Our love would be romantic
Full of touch and passionate kisses,
I would treat you gently my love
I shall respect you and your wishes.

Our lovemaking will be of beauty
We will reach the heights of elation,
Knowing our love was born in paradise
Each time will be a glorious sensation.

For to give to beauty is to love her
Treat her gently as a new flower in spring,
Smell her sensual perfume on her soft skin
Caress her and love her for she is everything.

She is your river of life that keeps you flowing
She is your laughter on a cloudy day,
A tower of strength to talk through your troubles
Your love everlasting to chase the blues away.

So love your woman, love her always
Be gentle and caring and kind,
Romantic, passionate and tell her you love her
That's the way to a woman's heart and beautiful
mind.

The Colour of My Life

I feel the existence of you
Like the heat of the sun,
Warm, passionate and beautiful
A tingling expectation of fun.

The smell of your perfume
The sweetness of your lips,
A wonderful feeling of love
Like a mature wine, I take sips.

Sips of your sweetness
You colour my life and my dreams,
I drink to the way you make me laugh
With your humour and themes.

At the dawn of each day
I love you for being my warm sun,
I love you for being who you are
Your smile makes each day everyone.

The Joy You Bring

Every time I see your smiling face
I thank the Lord for the joy you bring,
It makes me feel like a summer day
It makes me want to sing.

To sing the praises of the love we have
The beauty that embraces our being,
To smell the roses day or night
The colours the sight for seeing.

The elation the love that I feel
So precious is this sensation,
Within my heart and soul
So romantic so full of elation.

So full of summer so bright
So overwhelming tis true,
Such beauty I will caress forever
Because this love is for you.

This Is Love

You are a flower in a vase
That overflows in beauty,
The brightest star
In the midnight sky.
You, my love, are a treasure
That I embrace,
Even in my dreams
I kiss those beautiful lips.
For this and every feeling
Every breath that we share
Is full of pure love everlasting.
My senses overflow with joy
For you're the brightness
That fills my world with colour,
My rainbow of love and soul.
On this enchanted evening
I feel so much passion,
If this is love and feeling content
Then let this beautiful fulfilment,
This magical night, go on and on
In blissful, never ending love.

Under The Blossom Tree

She sings a beautiful song to me
Of faith and love and hope,
She says she wants to marry me
But I think we'll have to elope.

Cause this ''ere gal is only sweet sixteen
She's twenty years younger than me,
We fell in love most straight away
When we kissed under the blossom tree.

It was so romantic, her kisses are so sweet
I have never felt like this before,
I can feel the thud in my heartbeat
I love her, so, I just want more.

She reminds me of the moon
And stars that brightly shine at night,
She's got such a beautiful smile
She turns the darkness into light.

With her innocence and gentle touch
She is an angel sent from heaven,
So, I'm going to marry this little gal
And love her twenty, four seven.

Under The Heavens

I love the softness of your beautiful skin
I love your perfumed embrace,
I love everything about you my love
Including your cherry red lips to taste.

When we make love under the heavens
The stars float by in romantic motion,
What a beautiful setting in moonlight
As we sip the wine amid life's ocean.

Its wonderful darling, nature's bloom
The fragrance of the evening is sheer delight,
It makes you glad to be alive in the beauty
On such an enchanting summer night.

For in all the world there is nothing like it
It sets romantic hearts beating with love,
Such passion was given to us as a gift
Like this glorious evening from above.

Under The Stars

Let's dance to the music my sweetness
We'll have a night under the stars,
An open-air, concert in the garden
Whilst we look up to Jupiter and Mars.

It will be so full of romance and passion
A night to remember for all time,
Especially in the moonlight
Sipping a glass of champagne or wine

I'll highlight all the beautiful roses
I know your favourite colour is red,
The colour of your lipstick darling
I remember being smothered when we wed.

A wonderful evening the stars shine so bright
You can wear your evening gown my sweet,
With that necklace that sparkles with your eyes
You look so vivacious you'll be a princess
complete.

They danced in the moonlight to the lady in red
It was so romantic a fantasy dream come true,
And as they confessed their love for each other
They knew this night would last their whole
lives through.

Until The Stars No Longer Shine

Love me with all of your heart
Give me one of your red lip kisses,
Your sensual kisses drive me crazy
Full of passion and beautiful wishes.

For you taste delicious my darling
Let this night be never ending in love,
Your beauty is like the golden sun
I want to hold you my angel from above.

Hold you and keep you close to my heart
Look into your ocean blue eyes
And know this love isn't a sleepy dream
But a romantic scene under the bright skies.

The skies full of magical stars for lovers
To make all their wishes and dreams come true,
On this wonderful night my princess
For centuries they have shone on lovers like we
too.

We were made for each other the stars tell us so
Look at your surroundings the softness of the
night,
The perfumed rose petals as soft as your skin
The very nature of this world is a glorious sight.

I love you with every piece of my being
I will love you until the stars no longer shine,
I love you with so much passion in my heart
For you fill me with love which is simply divine.

Walking Through Her Dreams

Late at night when she goes
Walking through her dreams,
I lay and look at her beauty
So, content and at peace she seems.

There are no lines I can trace
Her baby skin so pure on her face,
And as she breathes so content
I kiss her lips so sweet to taste.

I love her with such passion
As she walks through her dreams,
I wonder where she is in these moments
She looks radiant in these angelic scenes.

I smile with so much happiness
Within my heart and soul,
For this is what she gives to me
This beauty makes me whole.

For she is all of my life
My sunshine, fun and treasure,
I will love her until the end of the world
Cause true love you cannot measure.

White As Snow

You looked at me with your beauty
Your face as white as snow.
Delving into my very being
Where I felt love that only you could know,
It was for you and only you,
My heartbeat pounded deep,
It was as if you knew all along
That it was yours to keep.
It was something between us that scared me,
It overflowed like nothing before.
It was filled with a feeling of pure elation
And we both knew the score.
Your sensuous body came closer
Your eyes were like the deep blue sea,
When our wet lips touched, I was powerless
To resist, you were like no other woman
I had ever kissed.
Your style I had to admire
In this brief moment
Life was a wonderful word.
Because love is for that moment
When everything else is oblivious and absurd.

Wonderful Feeling

Wonderful feeling
I love this feeling,
I'm on cloud nine
I'm on the ceiling,

When I'm with you
We can touch the skies,
I love you baby
I love your sweet sexy eyes.

I love your passionate
Romantic red lip kisses,
Your smooth, silk body
And your moonlight wishes.

I want to hold you forever
On the golden beautiful shore,
With our bodies wrapped in love
As we listen to the ocean roar.

With the romantic stars looking down
Making our future oh so bright,
This most wonderful feeling of love
With your beauty, makes everything just right.

Wonderful Spring Day

When daylight drifts through the window
And beauty lies sleeping at my side,
Gently I run my hand through her hair
As her eyes begin to open wide.

I kiss her voluptuous lips
Beside the bed I had placed fresh flowers,
She smiles as she whispers, I love you,
You can pamper me romantically for hours.

This love, this beauty, this setting
Could have come from a movie or book,
On this wonderful spring day
Love from her heart in a look.

Her angelic skin tasted so sweet
She was like a butterfly, soft and pure,
Lovemaking was so passionate
This was everlasting love and more.

I had never felt so much elation
Joy, happiness and sheer pleasure,
This angel this love this beauty
Will always be mine to treasure.

You Are My Rainbow

I love you and feel warm inside
You warm my heart like the sun,
The happiness that reflects
Between us is magical and fun.

There is no love so passionate
Our love is tender and sweet,
When I embrace you my love, my beauty
I want to kiss you from your head to your feet.

For in all the world you are my treasure
My angel of radiance, a picture divine,
You are my life, my love everlasting
You are my rainbow that makes everything fine.

Our romantic walks by the ocean
Our passionate love full of bliss,
Beautiful walks under the moonlight
Where we would blow the stars a kiss.

In the park the roses had a beautiful bouquet
With perfect peace, serenity and calm,
Oh, how we wished as we stared up at the stars
That this night would go on forever with all its
charm.

You Give To Me

You give to me the morning light of you
You give to me your loving smile,
You give to me your beauty day by day
You make my life worthwhile.

For it is in your beauty I can see
A picture glowing bright,
Of the purest love for one another
That makes our lives so right.

The romance and the passion
The thoughts of creativity flow,
The magic sewn together
Can only make our love grow.

The fun and laughter in life
The colour of our love,
Can only enhance the happiness
Given to us as a gift from above.

You Set Me On Fire

When I am alone with you
My love just increases,
You make me tremble
My heart rate goes to pieces.

That's what you do to me
You set my juices on fire,
With your passionate beauty
With your captivating desire.

Quench my love for you
Let these senses explode,
Let these beautiful souls
Combine together in loves hold.

For it brings me such elation
To hold your beauty in my embrace,
You are to me such a treasure
You are my jewel of loves face.

Forever my darling, let this be so
Look up, the romantic stars agree,
That to love and to be loved
Is harmony and true love for all to see.

Your Very Being

If you abide with me
I'll not forsake thee
I'll take thee to my breast

I'll love and teach you
The goodness I know
And bring you happiness.

As rivers flow in wisdom
I shall give thee life
In understanding.

The peace that dwells
Within your soul
Will be one of love.

Everlasting love
The joy you can behold
Within your heart.

Your very being
Will know elation
And peace as never before.